# DIVERSE SUPPLIER CONFERENCE

# **SUCCESS GUIDE**

Author:

Pamela Williamson, Ph.D.

Published by Alsky Social Marketing Firm

Email: contact@socialmarketingfirm.co

Website: www.asmf.co

ISBN: 978-1500993153

Printed in the United States of America

# Contents

# Introduction

## Why Attending Business Conferences Matters For Success?

Whether this is your first conference or your 50th, anyone can benefit from attending a business conference that is geared toward their field or subject of interest.

Perhaps you are looking to take a different career path or are looking to sharpen your skills and advance in the one you are established in. There is something for everyone to take advantage of.

The wise conference attendee is the one who is purposeful and focused, knowing exactly what they want to get out of their time away from the office and what kinds of fellow attendees that they'd like to network with.

It is our goal to help you learn what the conference attendance experts already know about how to make the most of your time at a business conference, how to capture as much information as you can and also, what to avoid if you want to reap all of the benefits that you should.

Grab a highlighter and some sticky notes, and drink in all that we have condensed into one concise "How To" for you to read and study before you ask for your name tag at the registration desk.

# CHAPTER 1

## What to Do When It Is Your First Time

# Hitting the Button

I Registered, Now What?

Sometimes the excitement of seeing that registration confirmation can soon give way to anxiety and uncertainty when it is your first time attending a business conference, especially if you are not going with a friend or coworker.

- Who will be there?

- What will I do in my downtime?

- Where should I stay?

- What do I bring?

These are just a few of the common questions that swirl around the mind of a new attendee, but you don't have to lose a minute of sleep over what it will be like and how you can go and enjoy your time and not feel like such a "newbie."

## Keep Calm by Preparing Your Strategy

Good planning is the key to feeling good about your conference attendance and will help you stay focused on why you are going in the first place. Business conferences are about gaining knowledge, learning who you need to familiarize yourself with in your industry, meeting other people in your space and networking with people that you can collaborate and do business with. To be sure, there is much to take in, but you need not overwhelm yourself with scattered thinking before you even set foot in the hotel lobby.

"Becoming well known (at least among your prospects & connections) is the most valuable element in the connection process."

- Jeffrey Gitomer

If you are traveling to an unfamiliar area, it can be stressful to figure out where you should be located while you are there. Not every conference is conveniently located in a hotel.

The first thing to do is check out any accommodation information that the conference website should have, listing out any details about special rates with neighboring hotels for registered attendees. Make an effort to try to stay in the hotel that is recommended if you can, since most of the attendees and exhibitors will be staying there as well. It is easier to network and spend time with others if you are all located in the same place.

If there are no special rates or if the hotel space set aside for the event is booked, then you will need to figure out where the next best place is to stay. This will take some traveler sleuthing, but it won't be hard to do.

- Call the venue and ask for suggestions

- Call the conference planner and ask if they have recommendations

- Use an online travel planner such as Expedia in conjunction with Google Maps to check the distance

- See what hotels can get you to where you need to go with public transportation

- If you are flying, consider a hotel that has shuttle service to/from the airport and event

Many sites like Expedia have even better rates than what may be offered through the event. It doesn't hurt to double-check "special rates" against what you can find online. AAA and American Express also offer their members premium discounts for travel as well. Check with them if you are a member of one or both of these.

# What Do I Bring?

## How to Pack With Purpose

Take it from many conference veterans before you, know what to pack and what to leave behind. Your body and your stress level with thank you for it.

### What Goes Into the Suitcase?

Keep in mind that your belongings will be wheeled and carried by you through a number of different places; airports, train stations, buses, even to and from the car or taxis. Compact is the keyword of the day when it comes to business conference travel.

Other than the necessary daily care items, comfortable clothes are a must. You will be sitting all day and walking around a large venue. Heels and suits are not advisable unless you are speaking or have a business networking event planned such as a Business Matchmaker Event planned for that specific day.

There are many fashionable, free-moving choices to consider when thinking about what is neat and professional-looking. It is also highly advised that you avoid anything that will require a lot of ironing. Think about fabrics that wear and hang well and that make you feel good about wearing them.

If possible, put things in one suitcase. It is best to select wardrobe pieces that mix and match. You'll get more wear out of them and have less clothing taking up space.

### Conference Gear to Bring

Now for what to pack into your tote bag for the conference. Less is more. Almost every conference will have notepads for you to use, if not, plenty of exhibitors and vendors give those kinds of things away. Pens will be ever available as well.

Bring business cards! You will definitely want to bring plenty of cards with you to hand out. Take a small supply of marketing materials with you as well to leave with those you make connections with. Your capabilities statement is an essential piece to networking and Business Matchmaker events. Make sure that they are included.

Do you really need that laptop? Most of the time, the tablets and laptops are better left at home or at least in your hotel room. They take up too much room and their weight isn't worth straining your back for the few minutes that you might happen to need it. Unless you have a presentation to do, leave it behind.

Instead of lugging a purse with you to the venue, take a small pouch to put your essentials in that will fit into a tote bag. It is one less thing to keep track of and won't take up as much space.

**Be sure and put in your pouch:**

- Your ID

- Any cash/credit cards

- Lipstick

- Hairbrush

- Medications

# Who Is Going?
## Knowing Who to Look For

Naturally, you want to know who will be speaking and what exhibitors you can find to speak to while you are there. You can find all of that on the event website. Oftentimes, additional speakers get announced, so check regularly. What is really important though is discovering what diversity supplier or procurement professionals will be in attendance that you would like to do business with.

### Check with Organizations That You Belong To

If you belong to any associations, ask if there are any members who will be in attendance alongside you. You may actually bring some interest to the membership base by asking if they are unaware of the event taking place.

If you are so inclined, ask who is going to the conference on your own Twitter handle and use the event's hashtag to see who responds. You can network with the responders as well and make some new connections in general.

### Check the Vendor List

Make sure that you are aware of who is sponsoring the conference and what exhibitors you will find there. You may have some close associations through business connections that you can leverage to make other connections.

# CHAPTER 2

## Good Time Management
## Staying in Control of the Clock

# How Many Workshops Should I Go To?

Make sure that you make time to attend every workshop that is relevant to your business and your ability to find new opportunities. Those are the ones that you don't want to miss out on.

Keynote speakers are usually well-known people with a lot of knowledge to offer so don't discount those. You can certainly get a lot of "take away" information from speakers of this caliber.

## Business Matchmaker Events

If you are in attendance to buy or sell a product or service during your time at your conference then you absolutely cannot afford to miss a Business Matchmaker event. These special events allow you the ability to sit in front of those who are looking to procure what you offer and tell them about how you can solve their current business issues. There can't be any better scenario to find yourself in at a conference. Make every effort to participate. It is as seamless a business networking vehicle as there could possibly be.

To find out more about Business Matchmaker events, see their informational page on their site.

# Using Social Media to Plan Your Schedule

**The Hashtag:**

Search on Twitter using the event's hashtag (For example: #WBECCONF) to easily sift through chatter for the specific event that you are attending. Start following the supplier diversity or procurement professionals on Twitter and see what they have to say about the event and what they will be looking to accomplish while they are in attendance.

This is also an opportunity to see what they Tweet about and the things they share with their followers. It will help you determine if what you offer is a right fit for what is going on in their business.

**What If They Don't Have Twitter?**

You can learn a lot about someone's professional background and their connections on LinkedIn. Even if the supplier diversity or procurement professional that you are interested in has a well-used Twitter account, check out LinkedIn as well. LinkedIn is an invaluable tool for doing your research and most importantly, seeing who you may know that is connected to the people that you are trying to network with.

Personal and corporate websites will have all the information you need to make your scheduling decisions as well. Read their blog posts to get a good idea of the kind of topics and talking points that they raise as business issues that you can help with.

There is no need to go into a networking event blindly anymore. There is plenty of information on the Internet to help you make the most of your time and schedule at your business conference.

# Networking before the Conference

You will have some great opportunities to network with like-minded business people by finding out who the followers of the speakers are that are attending. It is easy to find them:  They are usually talking about it on Twitter.

## Social Media for Better Connections

It's great to know what they find important about their favorite speakers and what their message is. It is also a nice idea to try and get to know some of them through social media and plan to meet up with them while you are there. Fellow attendees can also be business opportunities so don't overlook them. Try and come up with 5 to 7 good prospects for you to focus on that you have done a lot of research on beforehand. You will feel more prepared and purposeful about networking.

Some soft introductions are usually comforting when you are in a new place. If nothing else, you'll at least have some name tags to look for in the breakout sessions that you are both attending.

Follow the sponsoring companies of the event also. You can converse with the manager of their social media to find out any helpful information that you need to determine if their products or service are worth looking into while you are there. Networking is all about leverage. Use it to your advantage. The prepared and informed attendee is the one who usually gets the most of their time spent at a business conference.

# The Exhibit Hall and your Schedule

If there was ever a place where you can lose complete track of time and lose out on opportunities in which to learn and grow it's in the exhibit hall. With all the colorful booths and flashy props, it is easy to get dazzled and forget about the reason that you're there.

Unless you have procurement needs, there isn't a whole lot of time that should be spent there. Before you step into the exhibit hall, go on the event website and find out who will be exhibiting there. Make a note of the vendors that you want to meet with while you are in attendance and leave it at that.

## Keeping an Eye on the Time

You don't want to forget about the amount of time you need to discover new products and services while you are visiting the exhibit hall. Decide in advance how much time you will dedicate to visiting vendor booths and stick to it.

Make sure that you are not just running by booths to pick up pens and trinkets. Ask questions, engage with the exhibitors. They are there to help you understand their value. Take the time to get to know their businesses too, just like you would want someone to do for you.

Most conferences are more than one day. You don't need to visit every one in the same day. Space out your time and make sure that you are getting to the workshops and breakouts that you have planned.

# Take Time Out for New Connections

Make sure to make time for conversations with those that you want to network with. Ask to have coffee or sit at the same table at meal times. Get to know people and what their businesses are. That is one of the main reasons that you came, isn't it?

## Make Time to Take Time

You don't need to go to workshops just to go if they aren't what you need. If you find yourself with a gap in your schedule, ask one of your new connections to fill it with a meaningful conversation.

## New Connection Q&A

It is exciting to share with others what you do. One way that you can best help your new connection understand how you can help them with their business is to listen to what issues you can address.

Ask open-ended questions. Listen to details and encourage the other person to share complete information. Pay attention to what is said and make a mental note of what points you can help with through your business. You will both come away with a much more fruitful conversation.

# CHAPTER 3

## Good Conference Etiquette

# The Dos and Don'ts of Event Networking

The prospect of meeting new business connections is what it is all about. The nervous tension, the possibilities. It can throw you off your game, even if you are the most seasoned among us.

There is no need to panic. A few simple things to keep in mind will make establishing those new connections easy as pie.

**DO:**

Keep your business cards easy to reach

Keep mints handy

Find a simple open-ended question to start with

Put your cellphone on silent mode

Try to keep marketing materials as digital as possible for traveling professionals

**The Cocktail Party Scenario**

There is an easy way to help you measure your conversation; that is, know how not to dominate it. When you are excited, it is easy to over talk. Instead, encourage your new connection to do the talking.

When you are at a cocktail party, there is nothing more annoying than the partygoer who never stops talking about themselves. Think of the conversation like a volley. They ask a question, you answer, then you ask a question and listen. Keeping this mantra will keep the conversation going and make your new connection feel as though you are interested in what they have to say, not just collecting business cards.

**DO NOT:**

Check your cellphone repeatedly

Look around the room while someone is talking

Immediately start talking business opportunities

Approach a supplier diversity or procurement professional off-hours

Dominate the conversation or turn into an infomercial

You can talk about opportunities to do business a little later on in the conversation. The best business relationships are based on trust. You have to earn it, so don't jump the gun and ruin what could have been a fruitful business connection. Like any other relationship, it takes time to develop.

# Easy Ice Breakers

## Conversations with New People

Sometimes it is knowing what to say first that is the hardest part of beginning a conversation. If you are not good at breaking the ice, take heart, you are not alone.

Here are some tried and true examples of what to say to get your new connection talking:

*"Why are you interested in this conference?"*

*"What has been the best part of the event for you?"*

*"Anyone in particular that you came to see speak?"*

*"What are you looking forward to at the event?"*

These are examples of open-ended questions that require more than just a simple yes or no. If you want to get someone talking, ask them to offer an opinion on something. Remember to smile when they are talking and keep your attention on them. They're probably feeling awkward too. A smile is one of the most disarming things you can do to put someone and yourself at ease.

"My belief is that during conversations, it's not so much what you say, it's how you say it that matters. What's being heard is secondary to what's being seen, as body language leads the discussion and dictates the mood."

- Jarod Kintz, *This Book is Not for Sale*

# Business Cards

## The Seamless Exchange

This one can be tricky for a lot of people who are new to conference attendance. Knowing how to handle asking for a card with poise and confidence will get you better results and help you establish trust with your new connection.

There is nothing wrong with asking for one, but there is if you don't know how or when to ask.

### Don't Be a Salesman

The purpose of your trip is to find new opportunities, but there is something to be said for approaching the business card exchange with some finesse.

At times, someone will ask for your card as a way to end the conversation. Instead of just handing it over, use this technique instead.

*"Yes, let's exchange business cards so we can keep in touch."*

Did you see what happened there? Don't let them off the hook too easy. If yours is important enough to ask for, there is no reason for them not to give you theirs. If they don't/won't hand it over, it is very unlikely that they're serious about staying in touch with you.

Using that divine question can be utilized anytime. If you are interested in making a connection but are short on time, ask it another way.

*"I have to end this early but I do want to continue. Let's exchange cards and continue the conversation."*

This technique is easy, it's professional and it gets results. It is important to establish a conversation and some rapport with your new connection before you ask. Spend some time talking before you go for the ask.

# Difficult Personalities

## Handling Them Graciously

*"Every conference has a weird person in attendance. If you don't know who it is, it could be you."*

Not everyone you meet is going to have good communication skills. There are others with poor social boundaries that can leave you feeling awkward. Lastly, there are those who cross inter-personal lines and make you feel uncomfortable. There is a way to handle all of these situations without causing emotional injury to the other person not to mention, keeping your dignity intact.

**The Time Vampire**

This person seems unaware that there is an agenda for the conference and the fact that you might want to take advantage of it. If you give them one minute, they will take 2 hours. Be kind, but be firm.

"It was great talking to you, but I need to be at the next...."

Hold out your hand, smile, shake and tell them to enjoy the conference. The next thing you need to do is walk away. Otherwise, they will just keep talking.

## The Sob Story Teller

This is the one who volunteers too much personal information in too short a time and wants to suck you in to the drama of it all. Don't participate. They don't want advice, they want to console themselves with your listening ears.

"That *must* be hard."

Using that remark doesn't offer anything other than a comment. The next thing you need to do is use the first one, "It was nice to meet you, but I need to go to..."

## It Is OK To Not Be OK

If someone is making you feel uncomfortable in anyway; it is important to act on those feelings. You are feeling that way for a reason, respond to it. How you handle it can make a big difference to them and to you. If someone is just asking questions that are inappropriate, simply say that you'd prefer not to answer. If someone asks where you where you are from, respond with your general area, not your address.

If someone is making unwelcome advances or is harassing you in any way, you need to let them know that you are not okay with the conversation and walk away. If you are not feeling safe, let the conference staff know as soon as possible.

# Banquets and Happy Hour

## Negotiating Events with Alcohol

Attending parts of any event with a room full of strangers where alcohol is being served can be a dicey thing to navigate. People tend to over-drink when they are feeling uncomfortable, so keep that in mind both for yourself and for your fellow attendees.

### The Two Drink Maximum

You are representing you, your brand and your company. Be careful what you do when you involve alcohol. As a general rule; many savvy business people prefer to limit alcoholic consumption to two drinks at any event where business and pleasure are being mixed.

### Time Your Entrance and Exit

By all means, be social. It is important to do if you want to establish good business connections. You should consider this when you come and go from events that serve alcohol.

The best thing to do is show up on time and plan on leaving a half-hour early. For obvious reasons, the longer you stay, the more intoxicated that those who are around you become. You don't want to participate in becoming intoxicated or be known to associate. You have to be careful what happens in situations like this; your business reputation may depend on it.

### Knowing When to Discuss Business

Just because you see someone that you want to network with doesn't mean that it is the perfect time to discuss business. Approaching someone off-hours at the bar, the hotel lobby or the fitness center is not usually welcomed and is generally considered a pretty bad idea. There is a right time and a wrong time to present business solutions. Please let others enjoy their free time and privacy.

# CHAPTER 4

## Business Matchmaking Events

It's time for the big event. Are you ready?

# What Is A Business Matchmaker Event?

If ever there was a perfect situation for finding new opportunities with businesses that were looking to procure what you do, it would be a Business Matchmaking Event.

It is exactly what it sounds like. You participate in letting the supplier diversity or procurement professional know how you can solve their current business issues. It is all about offering a solution, not pitching features and benefits to products and services. This is your opportunity to shine in how you can do things better, faster or more efficiently than their current supplier.

Through procurement solutions like Cloud Custom Solutions, who developed the WBE platform specifically for the WBE community, what used to be a more complicated and longer task of finding new diversity supplier and procurement professional contacts has now become a more efficient, digital process through their Virtual Connection Corner. Now, research and introductions are seamless between buyer and supplier for a much more cohesive approach to business development.

## Think of the Possibilities

Wouldn't it be so easy and convenient to have meetings with people who are already interested in your product or service and lined up for you to meet with at an event or conference?

With Business Matchmaker, you can spend time doing what you do best: letting business know how you can solve their specific business issues. Does it get any easier than that?

# How Should I Prepare?

The most important thing that you can do in order to prepare for a Business Matchmaker event is to do your homework beforehand. The business leaders that participate as buyers at these events are looking for you to tell them why you should be their vendor of choice in your space.

You can't do that if you don't know what their pain points are and how you would alleviate them.

Take some time to peruse the business conference website and see what companies will be participating. Once you have the information, visit each and every website of the participating companies. Check their Twitter feeds as well. You are looking for news and events, open positions, office moves, corporate announcements, anything and everything that will give you some indication as to whether or not they are in need of your services.

## What They Are Not Looking For

Do not spend time putting together a canned, rehearsed slide presentation that is focused on *features and benefits*. The buyers do not want to know what you do as much as how what you do will solve their business issues.

Also, don't come to a Business Matchmaker event with a list of questions designed to help them tell you what they need. They want problem solvers not question askers. Be creative with the information on their website and solve the puzzle beforehand.

# What Happens At The Event?

It is normal to be a little nervous, but don't be. Everyone wants you to do well. After all, they are setting aside time for you, and they want to get the most out of it. So, relax. Just be prepared and you will do fine.

There are a couple of different scenarios that you may find yourself in, depending on the event set-up. You need to be prepared to make a salient point in either one of them. Don't forget your capabilities statement and business cards.

## One-To-One Meetings

Obviously, this would be your best option. Who doesn't want a solid, uninterrupted conversation with a supplier diversity or procurement professional who you know is looking to buy and has a high potential to need your services? You could have anywhere from 5 to 15 minutes to sit with your professional buyer. Be focused, smile let them know that you have done your research and are prepared to present a solution to a specific problem.

## Roundtable Meetings

In this situation you could sit at a table with a supplier diversity or procurement professional and 5 to 6 other suppliers who could offer anything related to your industry. They may or may not be a direct competitor of yours. They could also be potential strategic partners or even buyers. Don't overlook opportunity sitting at the table alongside you. Many great solutions come from more than one supplier. Look sharp and pay attention. You will only have about 2 minutes to present your company's solution.

# CHAPTER 5

## What to Do After the Conference

# Etiquette on Following Up

You won't even believe how fast it all comes to an end. It seems like just when you checked in to your hotel, 5 minutes later you were gathering up your things. As they say, "All good things come to an end." So it is with every wonderful conference.

## Maintaining Connections

It is important that you follow up with the business contacts that you established a rapport with while you were there. Keep those business cards in a safe place until you get home. Once you get settled back to your office, make sure that you personally email each one with an individually-directed message and sure to remind them briefly of what you talked about. Be sure and take notes on the back of their business cards to refresh your memory. While others may inundate them with emails right away, wait 2 or 3 weeks so that your email doesn't get lost in the shuffle. You may even want to ask your contact when would be a good time to reconnect. It is not recommended that you send communication through a third party such as your admin. They had the connection with you, not your office staff.

If now is not the right time for you to discuss an opportunity, follow up every 2 to 3 months with something relevant to talk about. Avoid the "I'm just calling to checkin" line. Have something to talk about that relates to their business, either on the news, in an article that you've read or based on something that you've gleaned from their website.

## Following Up

If you promised anyone that you would make sure that you connected them with someone or you said that you would email or forward any information to them, by all means do. Don't forget, it reflects poorly and no one remembers good intentions, just follow through. Write a note on the back of their card if it helps you remember.

# Notes, Slicks and Demos

If you are like most people, you stuff a whole ton of well-intentioned marketing materials into your conference tote bag with the very real hope that you would give each on a purpose in your business and a through read-through. Let's come back to reality...

## Mindful Gathering

While everything can sound intriguing while you are in front of a vendor in their booth, it is another thing to try and sift through all of the items that are being offered to you. Do you really intend to get that marketing slick to your operations department? Is that "latest and greatest" software something that you really were looking to buy? Don't get dazzled. A lot less is actually more. Your shoulders and recycling bin will thank you later.

## Demo and Sales Calls

The problem with leaving your card in that fishbowl to win a prize is that your card is now a lead for a salesperson to call on once they get back to their home office. Do yourself and them a favor and don't waste each other's time. Skip the prize drawing and avoid unnecessary sales calls that you don't intend to engage in.

# Passing on What You've Learned

Don't be afraid to share some great tidbits of information that you've learned with your team members or business association members. Information is best retained when it is passed on. Take notes and invite others to listen to what you took away from the conference.

## Taking Notes

If you intend to share your information with others or you were asked to bring back valuable insights to team members when you returned to the office, make sure that you are taking good notes. Write things down in an outline format to keep your thoughts organized. Transfer your handwritten notes to a typed document to share with others.

## Put Yourself in Their Shoes

Ask yourself a few questions when you are in your workshops. Try to imagine the kinds of things that someone would want to ask you if they weren't there to hear what you did. Ask yourself how the information relates to practical application at work. This will help you capture the right information for passing on to fellow team members.

# Proving ROI

This can be one of the most daunting tasks about coming back from a conference, but you need to honestly ask yourself what you gained from your attendance. Sometimes that is not realized for a few months. Your proof may come in the form of number of contacts you made and the kinds of valuable conversations you had.

**If You Are the Money Manager**

This will actually be harder than if you had to explain this to someone who is the steward over the company's finances. To the self-employed, a conference is a lot of expense if you don't understand what the return on investment should be for your business.

Some Simple Questions

- What was the final total for the conference spend?

- What is each contact worth in terms of business opportunity?

- What progress has been made in engaging in a viable opportunity?

- How long will it take to realize the opportunity monetarily?

- How many of those opportunities do you need to cover the cost?

- What opportunities would have been missed if you didn't go?

**Ask the hard questions before you are asked and you will be better prepared to answer.**

# What WBEC Is All About

WBEC is all about you, the woman-owned business. We strive to help you not only be the best that you can be, but also encourage you to align yourself with other world-class women-owned businesses both in your region and around the globe.

A WBEC certification sets your organization apart with a respected verification of your woman-owned status and adherence to best-practices that your buyers want to see when selecting an organization to work with.

## We Are Stronger As One Community

It is more than a logo on your website; your WBEC certification is your invitation to connect and develop relationships with other women-owned businesses. The relationships and business opportunities that our community has been able to develop *together* cannot be ignored.

WBEC's Virtual Connections Corner is a powerful online tool for establishing and growing relationship with our members. You can find out more about Virtual Connections Corner on our website.

Find out more about the WBEC certification today!

www.ingramcontent.com/pod-product-compliance
Lightning Source LLC
Chambersburg PA
CBHW050404180526
45159CB00005B/2146